Steffie
Out of the Box
Volume I

An inside peek at a fan's eclectic collection

Alison Boyd Rasmussen

Copyright © 2012 by Alison Boyd Rasmussen
Published by The Fashion Doll Review
PO Box 19851
San Diego, CA 92159-0851

All rights reserved. No part of this book may be reproduced in any form without the express permission of the author in writing except in the case of brief quotations in critical article and reviews.

Hello Kitty® is owned by Sanrio® Company Ltd..

Fashion Avenue® is owned by Newport News, Inc., a member of the Spiegel Group.

Miss America® is owned by the Miss America Organization.

BARBIE®, P.J.®, Christie®, Midge®, Whitney®, Cara®, Tracy®, Teresa®, The Heart Family®, Dolls of the World® and associated trademarks are owned by Mattel, Inc. Mattel did not authorize or approve this book, which is the author's own work. The opinions in this book are solely the opinions of the author, and do not reflect the opinions of Mattel or any other company.

For more information, contact the editor of The Fashion Doll Review at alison@fashiondollreview.com or www.fashiondollreview.com.

ISBN: 0983681635
ISBN-13: 978-0983681632

Dedication

This book is dedicated to Kathie Tilton, who has helped me add so many of these gorgeous dolls to my collection. There's always room for one more!

Who's that girl?

Standard Barbie redhead, European exclusive: This doll is very hard to find. She came on a hard plastic TNT body with straight legs, dressed in a blue swimsuit.

Why that girl?

I've been collecting Barbie since I was seven taking a short break in my twenties. As the years have passed, I've noticed a fondness for Mattel's Steffie sculpt.

Usually I look at the eyes when I choose dolls. However, a doll's mouth conveys emotion: happiness, passion, anger, confusion. Steffie's mouth is unusual, because it isn't exactly a smile. Her expression indicates she may be about to say something or kiss someone. This "about to" feeling makes her face so sweet and attractive to me.

Did you know that Steffie is the longest running sculpt in Mattel's lineup, and one of the most popular? Her versatility has kept her current over the years; her facial screening can be painted to make her eyes larger or smaller, and she has been manufactured in many different skin tones.

How to use this book

Welcome to the *Out of the Box* series. This book is the first in the series, and serves a single purpose: eye candy. I hope to provide Steffie fans with a casual visual reference of many wonderful dolls Mattel has produced, as well as inspiration for your own collection.

Please keep in mind that I am not a professional photographer, nor am I mint collector. I'm just a fan. My style is a little coarse and possibly even grungy. As always, feel free to contact me with any questions on my blog, the Fashion Doll Review: www.fashiondollreview.com. I try to respond to every comment. You can also email me at alison@fashiondollreview.com.

Walk Lively

One of only three dolls released with the Steffie name, Walk Lively was produced in the mod era. Don't confuse her with the more common Walk Lively Miss America, produced in 1972.

This lovely girl is dressed in her original outfit, plus an additional orange boa. I adore her metallic eyeshadow, similar to Free Moving and Deluxe Quick Curl P.J. of later years. She has rooted eyelashes and soft brunette hair.

She originally included a walking stand, red pilgrims, and a sash.

Busy Steffie

Also released in 1972, Busy Steffie came on the Busy Holding Hands body. When you raise and lower her arms, her hands will grip her various accessories.

She included a brown telephone, television, travel case, record player, and a tray with two glasses.

Malibu P.J.

P.J.'s violet eyes are highlighted in this dress by Integrity Toys. This version is Sunset Malibu, manufactured in Korea.

Many variants of Malibu P.J. are available for collecting. This girl shipped in a lilac swimsuit.

Check for subtle differences in eye color and paint, hair color, arm style, and country of manufacturer.

Olympic Gymnast P.J.

Similar in color and styling to Malibu P.J., Olympic Gymnast differs by her bright blue eyes.

She is more difficult to find than Malibu P.J., which makes her special.

Sun-Lovin' Malibu Christie

The tan lines say it all about this gorgeous doll. She included a cute pink bikini, aviator shades, and a beach towel.

Soft facial screening and casually styled hair is what made these beach-themed dolls popular.

The Sun-Lovin' series included two Steffie sculpts--both P.J. and Christie--in the lineup.

Sunsational Malibu Christie

Six years later, in 1984, Christie gets a little sportier in the Sunsational collection.

Again, both P.J. and Christie use the Steffie sculpt. Adding both to your collection is usually affordable.

Christie's hair can be a little thin when taken down from its original style, as shown in my photo.

Miss America

Originally available by mail order from Kellogg's, Walk Lively Miss America is a brunette Walk Lively doll with rooted eye lashes, dark blue eyes, and peach lips. Some dolls have longer hair.

This doll is dressed in a gown with a gold textured bodice and white nylon and net skirt, ermine-trimmed red cape. She included a Miss America sash, silver scepter, bouquet, and white pilgrims. She has a silver lace crown sewn into her hair. Earliest versions have a shorter crown than the one pictured here.

There was also a Walk Lively Miss America sold by mail order from Mattel in a pink display box. She included a walking stand and is more difficult to find.

Miss America Quick Curl Brunette

Once the Walk Lively dolls sold out, brunette Quick Curl dolls were sent as replacements.

They have brunette hair, eyes with painted eyelashes (not rooted), and a twist and turn body.

Quick Curl Miss America included the same outfit as Walk Lively: a dress with a textured gold lamé bodice, nylon and net white skirt, red cape with ermine trim, silver lace crown, scepter, bouquet, and white pilgrims. She included hair styling tools and accessories.

My doll has been restyled by Roberta Marino and is dressed in the wonderful pink version of Sweet Dreams.

Miss America Quick Curl Blonde

Quick Curl Miss America was released as a blonde beginning in 1975. She came in several variations:
- lace crown
- paper crown
- gold textured bodice
- gold lamé bodice
- silver lamé bodice
- ermine cape
- cape with a solid border

Boxed dolls also included curlers, comb, brush, ribbons, rubber bands, and bobby pins.

On this page, my violet-eyed girl has been carefully restyled by Roberta Marino and is dressed in the hard-to-find and ever-so-worth it Miss America fashion, Regal Red.

Miss America Quick Curl Blonde, version 2

This is a later version of Miss America, and believe it or not, one of the few dolls I have not removed from her box.

Notice her light blue eyes, pale blonde hair, and silver lamé bodice. Her cape has a solid white border. It has occurred to me that this solid border could be an end-of-the-fabric-bolt or selvage edge incident, rather than an actual variant.

However, there are several silver-bodiced dolls with solid white bordered capes in existence, and probably worth your persistent pursuit.

Quick Curl Kelley

Barbie's friend Kelley made her first appearance in 1973. She's a lovely strawberry blonde--and a Quick Curl, to boot.

Originally dressed in a green and white polkadot peasant style dress, Kelley is shown here in Velvet Venture.

Quick Curl P.J. Deluxe

With her super soft smile and dark eyes, Quick Curl P.J. Deluxe is sure to win your heart. What makes her "deluxe" is that she included additional long hair pieces to attach to her hairstyle.

Yellowstone Kelley

One of the most coveted Steffie sculpts, Yellowstone Kelley was originally produced in 1973. She can be pricey and difficult to find.

Her original outfit consists of a red polka dot blouse, striped shorts, knee socks, and tennis shoes. She's wearing a Best Buy fashion here.

Free Moving P.J.

Similar in screening to Quick Curl P.J. Deluxe, Free Moving P.J. has the same brown eyes and metallic eye shadow.

The Free Moving body has a latch in the back, which allows for additional posing opportunities. She included a tennis racquet and golf club as accessories.

She and Cara were released with the Steffie face in this collection.

Hawaiian Barbie

Hawaiian Barbie was a popular doll produced in several editions, beginning with a fine-haired 1975 version. Her facial screening, swimsuit fabric, and accessories changed with re-editions in 1977 and 1982.

This thicker haired girl is a 1982 version. Her hair is usually the fullest of the three, and her original swimsuit fabric uses the largest floral print. She is dressed in Collection Red Barbie Basic clothing and a scarf accessory.

My friend Milady Blue sent me this doll as a gift.

One of a Kind Hawaiian Barbie

This one-of-a-kind 1975 Hawaiian Barbie repaint and reroot is named Verusha. She was created by Lyna J. Grey of Barbie Resurrection in Parma, Italy.

I love her curled blonde hair and unique styling. She is definitely a unique doll in my collection.

Ballerina Cara
Released alongside the 1975 mod Barbie sculpt, Ballerina Cara included a special stand and ballerina body, which allowed her do kicks and splits.

Fashion Photo P.J.

A grail for many collectors, Fashion Photo P.J. is a pink box doll from 1978. These dolls can sell for $400 in never-removed-from-box condition.

Fashion Photo has medium brown hair with highlights, gorgeous brown eyes, and soft gold eyeshadow. She wears her original silver jumpsuit, aqua pants, aqua and green net coverup, and aqua t-straps.

Dolls of the World

Steffie was a popular sculpt for Mattel's Dolls of the World collection--you can see the versatility of her facial features and paint. I've included a few from this collection in the following pages.

Parisian

The first edition Parisian Barbie from 1979 has lovely starburst green eyes, a ribbon choker, and a bouffant style hairdo, upswept in a ponytail.

Parisian, second edition

In 1990, this doll was released as a second edition. Notice a few changes:
- slight change in hair color and style
- eyes are now blue and include lower lashes
- lips are brighter
- choker is plastic instead of ribbon
- a few details of the dress have also changed

Irish

The first issue in 1983 is the Steffie sculpt version. There are several variants of the Irish DOTW Barbie with subtle changes to her dress fabric and eye paint.

My Barbie is shown in her original outfit: an emerald satin dress with yellow trim, black velvet belt, white lace blouse with full sleeves, and a bonnet.

German

Released in 1986, this lovely doll wears a traditional German folk costume.

While the doll shown here is still in her box, I think this girl is particularly fun for redressing. Her pale blue eyeshadow makes a stylish 1980s era statement.

Peruvian

On the subject of blue eyeshadow, from 1985 is the Peruvian Doll of the World. She has gorgeous brown eyes, pink lips, and thick, long, dark braids.

India

An earlier Doll of the World issued in 1981, India is a fun collector's find. You can find her in two versions. First, in my photo: Her bodice is made from the gold net fabric you see here. This version has long black hair.

The second version has thicker brown hair, and her top is made from a gold lamé fabric, similar to the type used for Golden Dream's outfit.

The dolls' eye paint varies a little as well.

My recommendation: Add both to your collection and see which you prefer!

Black Barbie

Originally released in 1979 in a pink box with the phrase, "She's black! She's beautiful! She's dynamite!" on the front, Black Barbie originally included a sparkling red open shoulder dress with arm cutouts and gold accents on the front, and red accessories.

Here, she has been redressed in Beauty Secrets Barbie's outfit.

Black Barbie Reproduction

For her fiftieth anniversary, a reproduction of Black Barbie was released in 2009 as part of the My Favorite Barbie collection.

You can see subtle differences in facial screening and hair styling.

My doll has been redressed in a Fashion Avenue raincoat from 2001.

1980s Christie
Magic Curl

If hair play floats your boat, Magic Curl needs to be on your wish list. This adorable girl included a bottle of hair styling spray, providing for hours of styling opportunities.

The Caucasian version of this doll uses the Superstar face mold. Both dolls were released in 1982.

Golden Dream

Quick Curl hair made another appearance in 1981 with the Golden Dream dolls. Barbie uses the Superstar face, and Christie uses Steffie.

Not only did these dolls include new and improved styling accessories, but also disco-era mix and match outfits for endless restyling possibilities.

I'm in love with Christie's bronze hair highlights.

Pink & Pretty
Released in 1982, Pink & Pretty Christie was marketed for the outfit's versatility for play. The soft fuzzy pink boa and shawl could be styled as a skirt, cape, and hat.

1980s P.J.
Sun Gold Malibu

Bronzed skin, highlighted hair, natural makeup, and aviator sunglasses makes this 1983 doll worth a second look. Her green eyes are lovely, and make her harder to find than some dolls from the 1980s era, once removed from her box.

This doll's hair can be prone to an oily sheen and heaviness, due to the styling gel used to keep it place at the factory.

Dream Date

From 1982, Dream Date P.J. included a special skirt with a wrap-around boa, which could be styled in several ways.

As I child, I remember choosing Dream Date Barbie at the store, as P.J. had already sold out. My neighbor owned this doll, and I always envied her darker highlighted hair and blue outfit.

Barbie & Friends three-doll gift set

Identical in facial screening to Dream Date P.J., this doll is included in a set of three, with Barbie and Ken, dressed in casual clothing. She's wearing a navy and white sundress, tied with a fuchsia sash.

Sweet Roses
A soft pink skin tone, brunette hair, and a wonderfully pink petal skirt--Sweet Roses P.J. is another must-have for true Steffie fans and 1980s doll collectors alike.

Tracy Bride

With gorgeous brunette hair and emerald green eyes, Tracy made a one-time appearance in a high-necked lace wedding gown in 1983.

Here, her copious hair has been restyled in a retro side pony by Roberta Marino. She's wearing Pretty Changes Barbie's fashion.

This doll (like many dolls of this era) is prone to white or green blotches on her legs, due to aging of the plastic. While no treatment is known, I've heard of some collectors covering the spots with Magic Marker.

Her legs can also become sticky over time, and this stickiness can ruin clothing. A swap to a healthier body might be in order.

Whitney
Jewel Secrets

Whitney is known as Princess Laura in Europe. Jewel Secrets is another highly sought-after doll from the 1980s, especially in NRFB condition. Her lovely long hair is wonderful for restyling and play, and is often hard to find in good condition, once removed from the box.

Nurse

Always wonderful to see, Nurse Whitney has always enchanted me with her gorgeous teal eyes.

This doll not only included all sorts of medical accessories--stethoscope, scale, cast, otoscope, clipboard, watch, reflex hammer, blood pressure monitor, medicine bottles, note pad--she also included an evening outfit with a lacy blouse and pleated chiffon skirt. She could party all night after a grueling 12-hour shift at the hospital!

Midge
California Dreams

Barbie's vintage friend Midge cycled through the Steffie sculpt for just a few years in the 1980s era. Midge also went through the Diva, Mackie, and Teen Skipper faces.

Big hair, clashing earrings and neon Spandex define this girl. She included white roller skates and a Frisbee with her accessories. I love her green eyes and freckles.

Cool Times

Cool Times Midge included a popcorn bucket and pogo stick. This lovely auburn-haired girl has the 1980s era wall of bangs, huge earrings, and big blue eyes.

Both of these dolls can develop white and green spots on their legs, so examine them carefully before your purchase.

Teresa
Wet 'N Wild

Making her debut in 1988 using the Hispanic face mold as California Dream Teresa, Barbie's friend also used the Steffie face occasionally through the 1990s.

Besides her soft and fabulous hair--without the 1980s goop--Wet 'N Wild's swimsuit changes color when wet: from yellow and turquoise to green and purple.

Lights 'N Lace

Lights 'N Lace Teresa arrived in 1990 dressed in her peacock-themed lace outfit and cowboy boots. Oversized hair, earrings, a hair bow, and lace boot toppers can't be missed.

Her light is a giant belt buckle, which can be switched on and off. Mine still flashes dimly--much to the dismay of my ever-so-modern children.

Hispanic Barbie

Another collector favorite, released in 1979, this lovely doll was released as a European version called Rio Señorita.

There are at least two American versions: One has light brown eyebrows-- a variation of the one in my photograph.

Flight Time Hispanic

Big brown hair and a versatile day-to-night uniform, this wonderful doll has extra large eyes, quite typical of her 1990s era production year.

Fashion Play
1990

As the Fashion Play series were often less expensive, these dolls can be harder to find in good condition. Several Hispanic version of this series (but not all) use the Steffie face.

This doll usually sells for at least $40.

1991
This Fashion Play doll was released the following year. She is even harder to find than the 1990s version, but can sometimes sell for less--for between $25-30.

Special Expressions

Originally a part of the Fashion Play series, Special Expressions is an exclusive to Woolworth's, released in 1992. This girl often gets quite pricey--upwards of $50-100, depending on her condition.

I borrowed this doll from Lori Beth Lipkin of Happy Girl Gifts by Lori.

My First Barbie Ballerina

It was an utter delight was finding a Steffie-faced doll from the My First Barbie collection in 1991. She has soft hair, straight legs, and easy-to-change clothing.

What a perfect doll for a beginning collector!

Summit Barbie Hispanic

Another 1990s offering, the Hispanic version of Summit Barbie is a usually inexpensive find for the Steffie collector. Check out her fantastic starlit eyes.

Four dolls were offered in this collection, including African American, Asian American, and Caucasian versions.

Birthstone Beauties

The Birthstone Beauties collection included a different doll for each month's birthstone, in African American and Caucasian skin tones. Original dolls included a sparkling lace overlay cocktail dress, bolero, jewelry, and a miniature dog.

They are fun to restyle. Miss Pearl (June) has had her hair cut and styled by Elizabeth's Doll Spa. She's wearing a dress by Momoko and jacket by Integrity Toys.

Miss Amethyst (February) has been repainted and restyled by Lantis Kelley.

She was a gift from Kathie Tilton, who picked her up for me from the Italian Fashion Doll Convention.

Birthstone Beauties

The Birthstone Beauties collection included a different doll for each month's birthstone, in African American and Caucasian skin tones. Original dolls included a sparkling lace overlay cocktail dress, bolero, jewelry, and a miniature dog.

They are fun to restyle. Miss Pearl (June) has had her hair cut and styled by Elizabeth's Doll Spa. She's wearing a dress by Momoko and jacket by Integrity Toys.

Miss Amethyst (February) has been repainted and restyled by Lantis Kelley.

She was a gift from Kathie Tilton, who picked her up for me from the Italian Fashion Doll Convention.

Miss Peridot (March) is dressed in a one-of-a-kind outfit from Jennygrey and is wearing her original jewelry.

Miss Sapphire (September) is dressed in her original outfit, and she has had her curls softened.

My personal favorite of the collection is Miss Diamond (April), in her original outfit.

I recommend using caution when removing these dolls from their boxes. The hair can become a little frizzy.

Oshogatsu 1995

Two versions of Happy New Year Barbie were produced with the Steffie face in the mid 1990s.

The first version has long, dark hair, big brown eyes, red lips, and a red kimono.

Oshogatsu 1996

The second edition has shorter brown hair, soft pink lips, and a pink and gold kimono.

Forever Friends Reina

Anime fans might be enchanted with cutie Reina, a Japanese exclusive. Her brunette hair in ponytails, she is wearing a short schoolgirl style plaid skirt and carries a cellphone.

Fantasy Goddess of Asia

The only Bob Mackie to use the Steffie face (so far), this wonderful doll has a fantastical beaded gown, complete with embroidered dragon on a fan attached to her outfit.

Hello Kitty

Hello Kitty Barbie

The first in the series, these dolls included detailed themed accessories.

This doll has had her hair professionally styled by Designs by Robin Studio. She's wearing a blazer by Integrity Toys, and her velvet top and purse are by Mattel.

Hello Kitty Apple Tree

Another fun restyle by Designs by Robin Studio, this doll originally had her hair in a ponytail.

I love her upturned eyes and applies lashes.

She is wearing a trench coat by Integrity Toys and a vintage clone swimsuit.

Tarina Tarantino

Inspired by jewelry designer Tarina Tarantino, this gorgeous doll has rooted pink hair, applied lashes, and the most fabulous accessories.

Tokidoki Barbie

This Gold Label Barbie was an instant hit with no more than 7,400 dolls produced worldwide.

A short pink bob, skull jewelry, a spiky green pet named Bastardino, and controversial tattoos made this $50 doll fetch $400 and up on eBay!

Modern Circle Simone, Movie Premier

Dreamy eyes, highlighted green hair, and a shimmering green dress, Modern Circle Simone will bring a pop of color and a retro vibe to your collection.

Celebrate Disco

Released in 2008, this version of Celebrate Disco (often called Nikki) included a musical stand, that plays "Celebration."

Her sparkling gold and purple eye makeup and marabou outfit are really something!

Pop Life Redhead

A tribute to the mod era, the Pop Life collection includes several Gold Label dolls.

This doll uses the Pivotal body for easy posing. She is displayed in her box sitting on a pink chair.

I adore her applied eyelashes and pale pink lips.

Tribute Set, Matthew Sutton

From the 2009 Barbie Collectors Convention, this glamorous girl is one from the two-doll set, and was designed by Matt Sutton.

She has two-toned blonde hair, and an elegant bubble skirt cocktail gown with black lace overlay.

I love her simple, lash-free facial screening. It gives her a sleek, modern look.

Barbie Basics Model 03

2009 Collection 001

Making her debut as Model 03, Steffie appears as a brunette with bangs and beautiful blue eyes.

Originally in a simple knit dress, my doll is wearing a 001.5 Basics outfit with sunglasses by Integrity Toys.

2010 Collection 001.5

A little more upscale than the original black knit dresses, the 001.5 Barbie Basics Collection used black satin with pink bow accents and belts.

Model 03 has red curls and glamorous shimmering makeup. She's been redressed in an outfit by J-Doll (Groove). Her accessories are from Barbie Basics accessories pack Look 002, Collection 001.

2010 Collection Red

Released as one of three exclusive dolls for Target's first Collection Red, Model 03 is displaying a few accessories from the exclusive Target set.

2011 Collection 002

Collection 002 Barbie Basic dolls swapped cocktail attire for jeans and tees. Accessories sets--Look 001 and Look 003, shown here--from the same collection add a little sparkle.

2011 Collection
Red
One of the three dolls released for Target in 2011, this rockabilly styled Model 03 reminds me of singer Katy Perry.

Versatility of Basics

Doll artists were thrilled to see basic Model Muse bodies at reasonable prices for custom work.

This is a repainted and rerooted 2010 001.5 Collection Model 03, created by doll artist Crushed Velvet Orchid.

Standard Canadian Barbie

Another collector secret: Canadian Standard Barbie from the mid 1970s! She is usually found with blonde or strawberry blonde hair, blue eyes, and a pale straight leg plastic body.

Her hair can be a little thin, and her face can be prone to faded spots, so choose carefully. Lip and eye paint varies from doll to doll.

Not only was the Canadian Standard available in a pink or blue swimsuit, she also came dressed in a variety of Best Buy outfits. These dolls can be hard to find, but they are worth the effort.

I think of it as a treasure hunt!

Heart Family Mom

Did you know that the African American version of Mattel's Heart Family mom uses the Steffie sculpt? She varies widely in her facial screening and is oh-so-lovely.

This version is from 1984, and is called Mom and Baby. She wears a pale pink drop waist dress with a large lace collar.

Partytime Barbie

A personal grail doll, Partytime Barbie was released as a European exclusive in 1977. She has rose gold eyeshadow and rooted eyelashes. Originally, she was dressed in a dress with gold lamé bodice with an orange and gold lace overlay skirt.

There were four versions released around this time, all called Partytime. One used the mod Barbie face and wore the same orange and gold dress. The other used the Superstar sculpt and wore a red bodice dress with a black floral skirt in a similar style. Finally, there was a second Steffie released in the red/black floral dress as well.

All four dolls have rooted eyelashes and similar facial screening.

Activa by Cipsa

Another fabulous restoration by the talented Roberta Marino, Activa was created by Cipsa in Mexico, which Mattel licensed in the mid 1970s.

My version has darker painted lips from the original's nude color, but her large pupils and eyelashes are a trademark of this girl. She is dressed in Dreamy Pink.

More Information About Steffie

I have done a little research on which dolls have been manufactured by Mattel in the US using this gorgeous sculpt. I don't believe this is a complete list--but I'm sure it will be a good reference, as well as a good start to your collection.

Year	Name	Doll	Notes
1972	Malibu	P.J.	
1972	Walk Lively	Steffie	
1972	Busy	Steffie	
1972	Talking Busy	Steffie	
1973	Quick Curl	Kelley	
1973	Walk Lively	Miss America	
1973	Quick Curl	Miss America	
1974	Baggie doll, #7888	Babs	Same as Busy Holding Hands, without accessories
1974	Yellowstone	Kelley	
1974	Quick Curl	Miss America	Blonde or brunette
1974	Free Moving	P.J.	
1975	Hawaiian	Barbie	There are three versions of Hawaiian Barbie, all slight variants
1975	Free Moving	Cara	
1975	Quick Curl	Cara	
1975	Gold Medal Olympic Gymnast	P.J.	Available singly or in a set
1976	Ballerina	Cara	
1976	Quick Curl Deluxe	Cara	
1976	Quick Curl Deluxe	P.J.	
1977	Hawaiian	Barbie	
1978	Fashion Photo	P.J.	A collector favorite!
1978	Sun Lovin' Malibu	P.J.	
1979	Hispanic	Barbie	
1979	Parisian	Barbie	Both 1979 and 1990 editions are Steffie faces.
1979	Sun Lovin' Malibu	Christie	
1979	Heart Family AA	Mom	Heart Family

Year	Name	Doll	Notes
1980	Black	Barbie	There was a reproduction of Black Barbie in 2009 for Barbie's 50th birthday.
1981	India	Barbie	
1981	Golden Dream	Christie	
1982	Hawaiian	Barbie	
1982	Magic Curl AA	Barbie	
1982	Pink and Pretty	Christie	
1982	Sunsational Malibu	Christie	
1982	Barbie and Friends 3-doll gift set	P.J.	This doll has the same facial screening as Dream Date P.J..
1982	Dream Date	P.J.	
1982	Sunsational Malibu	P.J.	
1983	Irish	Barbie	
1983	Native American Convention Doll	Barbie	Hispanic version
1983	Sun Gold Malibu	P.J.	
1983	Sweet Roses	P.J.	
1983	Bride	Tracy	
1984	Heart Family and Baby AA	Mom	Heart Family
1985	Peruvian	Barbie	
1985	Heart Family New Arrival AA	Mom	Heart Family
1986	Feelin' Groovy (Billy Boy)	Barbie	
1986	German	Barbie	
1986	Heart Family Birthday Surprise AA	Mom	Heart Family
1986	Heart Family Kiss & Cuddle AA	Mom	Heart Family
1987	Heart Family Bathtime Fun AA	Mom	Heart Family
1987	Heart Family Schooltime Fun AA	Mom	Heart Family
1987	Jewel Secrets	Whitney	
1988	California Dream	Midge	
1988	Heart Family Visits Disneyland AA	Mom	Heart Family
1988	High School	Stacie	Jazzie's (Barbie's cousin) friend
1988	Nurse	Whitney	
1988	Perfume Pretty	Whitney	
1989	Cool Times	Midge	

Year	Name	Doll	Notes
1989	Style Magic	Whitney	
1990	Fashion Play Hispanic	Barbie	White and lavender lingerie
1990	Flight Time, Hispanic	Barbie	
1990	Parisian second edition	Barbie	
1990	All Star	Teresa	
1990	Wet 'n Wild	Teresa	
1991	Fashion Play, Hispanic	Barbie	
1991	My First, Hispanic	Barbie	
1991	Summit Barbie, Hispanic	Barbie	
1991	All American	Teresa	
1991	Lights & Lace	Teresa	
1992	Fashion Play, Hispanic	Barbie	
1992	Spanish second edition	Barbie	
1992	Special Expressions (Pink Dress)	P.J.	Woolworth's exclusive
1994	Western Stampin'	Tara Lynn	
1996	Oshogatsu (Happy New Year Japanese)	Barbie	
1997	Oshogatsu (Happy New Year Japanese)	Barbie	
1998	Birthday Party	Barbie	Blonde, brunette, and African American
1998	Fantasy Goddess of Asia (Bob Mackie)	Barbie	So far, this is the only Steffie sculpt Bob Mackie has used.
2003	Modern Circle, Make-Up Artist	Simone	
2004	Paul Frank	Barbie	Red and blue pajamas
2004	Modern Circle, Movie Premier	Simone	
2007	Birthstone Beauties, AA	Barbie	January-December, there were twelve of each of these dolls in the series.
2007	Birthstone Beauties, Caucasian	Barbie	
2007	Hello Kitty	Barbie	
2007	Top Model Premier	Summer	
2007	Top Model Resort	Summer	
2007	Top Model Resort, Hair Wear	Summer	
2008	Hello Kitty Apple Tree	Barbie	Toys R Us exclusive
2008	My Melody	Barbie	
2008	Tarina Tarantino	Barbie	

Year	Name	Doll	Notes
2008	Celebrate Disco	Nikki	
2009	Black Reproduction	Barbie	
2009	Tribute Giftset, Matthew Sutton	Barbie	National Collectors Convention, blonde
2009	Pop Life Redhead	Kelley	
2009	Basics 001 Model 03	Barbie	
2010	Basics 001.5 Model 03	Barbie	
2010	Basics Collection Red Model 03	Barbie	Target exclusive
2011	Basics 002 Model 03	Barbie	
2011	Basics Collection Red Model 03	Barbie	Target exclusive
2011	Tokidoki	Barbie	
2012	City Shopper	Barbie	Steffie version, blonde with eyelashes

Additionally, I'd encourage you to look for foreign issue Steffie dolls. Here are a few to consider:

Year	Name	Doll	Notes
1975	Standard, TNT body, hollow plastic	Barbie	Australian exclusive, titian, blonde, and brunette hair
1976	Standard TNT in Bicentennial dress	Barbie	Australia, blonde, dressed in Best Buy
1976	Standard TNT in red dress	Barbie	Australia, blonde, dressed in Best Buy
1973	Standard, TNT body, hollow plastic	Barbie	Canadian exclusive, blonde in swimsuit
1977	Standard TNT in pink dress	Barbie	Canadian exclusive, blonde in Best Buy
1977	Standard TNT in red print dress	Barbie	Canadian exclusive, blonde in Best Buy
1977	Standard TNT in yellow shirt, red jumper	Barbie	Canadian exclusive, blonde in Best Buy
1977	Standard TNT in red shirt, plaid trousers	Barbie	Canadian exclusive, blonde in Best Buy
1980	Hollow body TNT, green dress	Barbie	Canadian exclusive, blonde in Best Buy
1980	Hollow body TNT, Partytime dress	Barbie	Canadian exclusive, blonde in Best Buy
1980	Hollow body TNT, Pretty Changes outfit	Barbie	Canadian exclusive, blonde in Best Buy
1980	Hollow body TNT, red fringed dress	Barbie	Canadian exclusive, blonde in Best Buy
1980	Hollow body TNT, gold lace dress	Barbie	Canadian exclusive, blonde in Best Buy
1980	Hollow body TNT, yellow floral dress	Barbie	Canadian exclusive, blonde in Best Buy
1980	Hollow body TNT, Royal dress	Barbie	Canadian exclusive, blonde in Best Buy
1987	Club California	Midge	Canadian exclusive, variant of California Dreams Midge, includes cassette tape

Year	Name	Doll	Notes
1976	Partytime	Barbie	European exclusive, gold/orange dress
1976	Partytime	Barbie	European exclusive, red/black dress
1991	Benetton	Teresa	European exclusive
1992	Benetton Shopping	Teresa	European exclusive
1992	Ultra Hair	Whitney	European exclusive
1974	Standard, TNT body, hollow plastic body	Barbie	Europe, blonde, blue swimsuit
1975	Standard, TNT body, hollow plastic	Barbie	Europe, blonde, pink swimsuit
1979	Ebony	Christie	Europe, variant of Black Barbie
1979	Rio Señorita	Barbie	Europe, variant of Hispanic Barbie
1992	Heart Family Mom & Baby	Mom	India, made by Leo, same outfit as US version, Caucasian with blonde hair
1981	Réve d'Or Da Sogno	Christie	Italian variant of Golden Dream, her arm bands are bronze lamé
1999	Forever Friends	Reina	Japan exclusive
2008	Vidal Sassoon 60s, Platinum Label	Steffie	Japan promotional doll, LE 300
2008	Vidal Sassoon 70s, Platinum Label	Steffie	Japan promotional doll, LE 300
1983	Bride	Tracy	Mexico only, variant of Tracy, bodice lace is different, eyes are olive green, very pretty eye paint
1987	Barbie Noiva	Viky	Made by Estrela in Brazil, bride outfit
1988	Cor do Verão	Viky	Made by Estrela in Brazil, "Color of Summer"
1989	Rock Star	Viky	Made by Estrela in Brazil
1989	Viky Passeio	Viky	Made by Estrela in Brazil - also given to Barbie Convention attendees
1989	Moda Festa	Viky	Made by Estrela in Brazil, "Fashion Festival"
1990	Amigos de Selva	Viky	Made by Estrela in Brazil, "Jungle Friends"
1991	Primavera Verão	Viky	Made by Estrela in Brazil, "Spring Summer"
1991	Esporte Total	Viky	Made by Estrela in Brazil, "Total Sport"
1992	Festa de Casamento	Viky	Made by Estrela in Brazil, "Wedding Party"
1994	Arte em Moda	Viky	Made by Estrela in Brazil, two-doll set, variant of Paint n' Dazzle
1989	Moda em Dobro	Lia	Made by Estrela in Brazil, "Fashion in Double"
1989	Alta Costura	Lia	Made by Estrela in Brazil, "Haute Couture," at least two fabric variations

Year	Name	Doll	Notes
1989	Laço de Perfume	Lia	Made by Estrela in Brazil, variant of Perfume Pretty with lighter hair and different dress
1989	Rock Star	Lia	Made by Estrela in Brazil - there are many versions of Lia available
1991	Outono Inverno	Lia	Made by Estrela in Brazil, "Autumn Winter"
1989	Bruna - Tênis & Jeans	Teresa	Made by Estrela in Brazil, variant of All American Teresa
1994	Country	Tina	Made by Estrela in Brazil, variant of Western Stampin' Tara Lynn
1987	Laura Fragancia	Whitney	Made by Congost in Spain, variation of Perfume Pretty
1986	Princess Laura	Whitney	Made by Congost in Spain, variation of Jewel Secrets Whitney
1983	Bride	Tracy	Made by Aurimat in Mexico, another variant with exaggerated lower lashes
1975	Peinado Magico, blue blouse	Barbie	Made by Cipsa in Mexico, Quick Curl
1975	Peinado Magico, green blouse	Barbie	Made by Cipsa in Mexico, Quick Curl
1975	Activa	Barbie	Made by Cipsa in Mexico
1977	Modelo	Valerie	Made by Cipsa in Mexico
1978	Tahitiana	Valerie	Made by Cipsa in Mexico
1978	Hollywood	Valerie	Made by Cipsa in Mexico
1990	Hawaiian Fun	Kira	Made by Rotoplast in Venezuela
1991	Glitter Beach	Teresa	Made by Rotoplast in Venezuela
1989	Wet 'n Wild	Withney [sic]	Made by Rotoplast in Venezuela
1991	Luces y Encaje	Teresa	Made by Rotoplast in Venezuela, Lights & Lace variant
1988	Career Barbie	Whitney	Made by Richwell in the Philippines

Cipsa, Rotoplast, Congost, Aurimat, and Estrela were licensed by Mattel. Additionally, you might also be able to find more Steffie sculpts created by Richwell (Philippines), LEO (manufactured in India), Plásticos Gloria (Chile), and BASA (made in Peru). I've seen a blonde Steffie-faced BASA doll from the 1980s with bent arms. She was nude, so I'm not sure of her name.

In the mid 1970s, Dutch company Tomfu-Nekmer manufactured dolls modeled closely after Yellowstone Kelley called Super Linna. They are probably not licensed by Mattel. They are fairly high quality and can be hard to find.

Steffie References

Check out the following websites for some great online references.

http://www.flickr.com/groups/751348@N24/
Flickr photo group dedicated to the Steffie sculpt

http://steffiedolls.wetpaint.com/
A Wiki set up for Steffie sculpts

http://www.fashion-doll-guide.com/Steffie-Doll.html
Fashion Doll Guide's reference

http://www.kattisdolls.net/facemold.htm
Katti's Dolls face mold reference site

http://bricio-pires.blogspot.com/
A really helpful blog about hard-to-find Estrela Barbies.

http://www.michaelaugustyniak.com/
Specifically, the *Barbie® Doll Around the World* book, published in 2008 by Collector Books, is a fantastic resource for those hard-to-find and rare Steffie sculpts.

Resources

You can find the following manufacturers and OOAK artists in my photos:

Artist Name	Contact
Barbie Collector	http://www.barbiecollector.com
Barbie Resurrection Lyna	http://www.facebook.com/L.J.GreyBarbieHospital
Crushed Velvet Orchid	http://thedollaffinity.blogspot.com
Designs by Robin Studio	http://shop.designsbyrobinstudio.us
Elizabeth's Doll Spa	http://dollspa.webs.com
Groove Inc.	http://groove.ws
Happy Girl Gifts by Lori	http://stores.ebay.com/happygirlgiftsbylori
Integrity Toys	http://www.integritytoys.com
Jennygrey	http://jennygrey.etsy.com
Kathie's Fashion Dolls	http://stores.ebay.com/kathiesfashiondolls
Lantis Kelly	http://lantis-kelly.com
Mattel	http://www.mattel.com
Momoko	http://www.petworks.co.jp
Sanrio	http://www.sanrio.com
Target	http://www.target.com
Tokidoki	http://www.tokidoki.it

Thanks for allowing me to feature your wonderful dolls and outfits in this book. Thanks especially to Lori Beth Lipkin for lending me her lovely Special Expressions Barbie.

I am in no way affiliated with these companies. I'm merely a fan, who thinks you should support these companies and artists with your wallets.

You can always find me at my blog, The Fashion Doll Review: http://www.fashiondollreview.com, where I am always happy to receive your friendly comments.

No part of this book may be reproduced without permission.

www.ingramcontent.com/pod-product-compliance
Lightning Source LLC
Chambersburg PA
CBHW042001150426
43194CB00002B/81